¡Sí, Se Puede!

Yes, We Can!

written by **DIANA COHN**

illustrated by **FRANCISCO DELGADO**

essay & poem by Luis J. Rodríguez

Janitor Strike in L.A.

for Kathryn~
Thank you for all
you are doing to
make the world a
better place!
¡Sí Se Puede!
Diana

"**SLEEP WITH THE ANGELS,** Carlitos," says Mamá when she tucks me in.

"See you in the morning," I say and close my eyes.

While everyone sleeps, my mamá goes to work. She rides the bus into downtown Los Angeles where skyscrapers shoot up from the sidewalks. At night, the streets are empty.

—QUE SUEÑES CON LOS ANGELITOS, Carlitos, —dice mamá cuando me tapa con las cobijas.

—Hasta mañana—le digo y cierro los ojos.

Mientras todo el mundo duerme, mi mamá va al trabajo. El autobús la lleva al centro de Los Ángeles donde los rascacielos se alzan de las aceras. Por la noche, todas las calles están vacías.

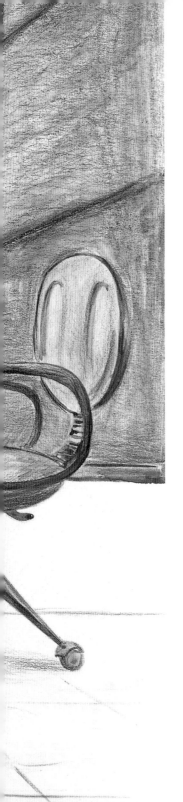

IT'S QUIET when my mamá goes into the tall glass office building where she scrubs the bathroom tiles so they shine like the moon, cleans the tall glass windows so they are as clear as the lake where my papá taught me to swim, and mops and polishes the floors so smooth you can slide on them if you take off your shoes.

After that, she sorts and dumps all the trash. The sun is ready to rise when she takes the bus back home again to me.

TODO ESTÁ SILENCIOSO cuando mi mamá entra en el alto edificio de oficinas de vidrio donde ella friega los azulejos de los baños hasta que brillan como la luna, limpia las ventanas altas de cristal hasta ponerlas tan claras como el lago donde mi papá me enseñó a nadar, y limpia y les da brillo a los pisos hasta que quedan tan lisos que podrías deslizarte por ellos si te quitaras los zapatos.

Luego, separa y tira toda la basura. El sol está a punto de salir cuando ella sube en el autobús para volver a casa y a mí.

WHEN I WAKE UP, Mamá is always in the kitchen talking to my abuelita. We all eat breakfast together. Abuelita fixes me a bean burrito for my lunch. When I'm ready, Mamá walks me to the school bus.

"Sleep with the angels, Mamá," I call out the window.

"Have a good day at school," she says. Then she goes back home to bed.

CUANDO ME DESPIERTO, mamá siempre está en la cocina hablando con mi abuelita. Nos desayunamos juntos. Mi abuelita me prepara un burrito con frijoles para el almuerzo. Cuando estoy listo, mamá me acompaña a la parada del autobus escolar.

—Que sueñes con los angelitos, mamá—le grito desde la ventana.

—Que la pases bien en la escuela—dice. Entonces vuelve a la casa a dormir.

7

ONE NIGHT Mamá said, "Do you know, Carlitos, I can't take care of you and your abuelita the way I want to."

She sat me on her lap to explain.

"Even though I work full time as a janitor, I also have to clean houses and wash clothes on the weekend. That means we don't have any time together. And I can't afford to buy the medicine Abuelita needs to help her sore bones feel better."

I looked at my abuelita. I looked at my mamá. I looked at the family photos on the wall. My favorite was the one of her dressed in her wedding gown with my papá. When Papá was still alive we all lived in Mexico, the country where I was born.

UNA NOCHE, mamá me dijo:—¿Sabes, Carlitos? No puedo cuidarlos a ti ni a tu abuelita como quisiera.

Me sentó en sus rodillas para explicármelo.

—Aunque trabajo tiempo completo como conserje, también tengo que limpiar casas y lavar ropa los fines de semana. Por eso no tenemos tiempo juntos. Y aun así no tengo dinero para comprar la medicina que la abuelita necesita para que no le duelan los huesitos.

Miré a mi abuelita. Miré a mi mamá. Miré las fotos de familia en la pared. Mi favorita era la de ella vestida de novia con mi papá. Cuando papá vivía todavía, todos vivíamos en México, el país donde nací.

"CARLITOS," she said, "to work so hard and get paid so little isn't fair. So today, all the janitors met outside the union hall and voted to stop working…to strike! We're going to let those offices get dirtier and dirtier and won't clean them again until we get the pay raises we deserve."

"But Mamá, can you do that?" I asked.

"That's just what I asked," she said. "Can we do this? And all the janitors shouted back at the same time, 'Sí, se puede! Yes, we can!' So tomorrow we're going on strike.

"And Carlitos," Mamá said as she combed her fingers through my hair, "for me to put my full heart into this, I am going to need your help."

I hugged my mamá. "I'll help you," I said. But in bed that night, I couldn't think of what I could do.

—CARLITOS —dijo—, trabajar tanto para ganar tan poco no es nada justo. Entonces hoy todos los trabajadores de limpieza nos reunimos afuera del local del sindicato y votamos por parar de trabajar… ¡nos declaramos en huelga! Vamos a dejar que las oficinas se pongan cada vez más sucias, y no las limpiaremos hasta que no nos aumenten el pago como merecemos.

—Pero, mamá, ¿se puede hacer eso? —le pregunté.

—Eso lo pregunté yo también—dijo—.¿Se puede hacer esto? Y todos los trabajadores juntos respondieron a gritos, '¡Sí, se puede!' Pues mañana, vamos de huelga.

—Y Carlitos—me dijo mamá mientras me pasó los dedos por el pelo—, para que yo la haga de todo corazón, es necesario que tú me ayudes.

Abracé a mi mamá. —Yo te ayudo—dije. Pero en la cama esa noche, no pude imaginarme qué podría hacer yo.

THEN THE STRIKE BEGAN. Mamá and all the other janitors marched, held rallies and had lots of meetings. Our phone never seemed to stop ringing.

Every morning, Mamá read me newspaper articles about the strike. She showed me photos of bus drivers, carpenters, ministers and students, all marching alongside the janitors.

"Where did they all come from?" I asked.

Mamá's eyes lit up. "So many people promised to help us. People from Los Angeles and from all over California and even from other states came to take a stand with us."

ENTONCES EMPEZÓ LA HUELGA. Mamá y todos los otros trabajadores de limpieza manifestaron, hicieron mítines, se reunieron mucho. Nuestro teléfono no parecía dejar nunca de sonar.

Cada mañana mamá me leía artículos del periódico acerca de la huelga. Me mostraba fotos de choferes de autobuses, carpinteros, sacerdotes y estudiantes, todos marchando al lado de los trabajadores.

—¿De dónde vinieron todas estas personas?— pregunté.

Los ojos de mamá se iluminaron. —Tanta gente nos prometió su ayuda. Gente de Los Ángeles y de todas partes de California y hasta de otros estados vino a solidarizarse con nosotros.

I CUT OUT THE PHOTOS to bring to school. Then I found out I wasn't the only one in my class with a parent on strike. Maria's father is also in the union; they're from El Salvador. And Tino's mother, who's from Nicaragua, was out at the marches every day too. Our teacher, Miss Lopez, told our class that when her grandfather came to the United States, he was also treated very badly, just as if he wasn't a person!

"Grandpa and the other farmworkers joined together to fight for a better life—just like the janitors are doing now."

"Did they win?" I asked.

"You bet they won! When many people join together, they can make a strong force."

RECORTÉ LAS FOTOS para llevármelas a la escuela. Entonces me di cuenta de que no era el único en mi clase que tenía familiares en huelga. El papá de María también está en el sindicato. Son de El Salvador. Y la mamá de Tino, de Nicaragua, iba todos los días a las manifestaciones también. Nuestra maestra, la señorita López, nos contó a la clase que cuando su abuelo vino a los Estados Unidos, lo trataron mal también, '¡como si no fuera un ser humano!'

—El abuelo y los otros trabajadores agrícolas se juntaron para luchar por una vida mejor, como lo están haciendo los trabajadores de limpieza ahora.

—¿Y ganaron? —le pregunté.

—¡Claro que sí! Cuando mucha gente se junta, puede tener mucho poder.

MAMÁ TOLD ME lots of different stories about the strike.

"So many people have come to support us. Today a man came out of his building to join our rally. He said he'd never thought about the janitors who clean his office. 'But seeing you in the bright light of day,' he said, 'means I can never ignore you again.'

"And this afternoon even Miss Lopez was there. As the sun set, we stood together and held candles in our hands. And in that silence, we didn't feel how tired we were from marching all day...instead we felt the glowing light of our strength."

MAMÁ ME CONTÓ varias historias acerca de la huelga.

—Muchas personas han venido a apoyarnos. Hoy un hombre salió de su edificio para participar en nuestra reunión. Dijo que nunca había pensado en la gente que hace la limpieza de su oficina. 'Pero al verlos a plena luz del día,' dijo, 'jamás podré olvidarlos.'

Y esta tarde hasta la señorita López estaba allí. Al ponerse el sol, nos quedamos parados con velas en la mano. Y en este silencio, ya no sentimos el cansancio por haber marchado todo el día...más bien sentimos la luz radiante de nuestra fuerza.

17

THE NEXT NIGHT I saw my mamá on the news, making a speech! Hundreds of people were marching behind her. That's when I knew what I could do to help. I'd go downtown, too...but with a special surprise.

A LA NOCHE siguiente, ¡vi a mi mamá en las noticias, dando un discurso! Cientos de personas manifestaban detrás de ella. Fue entonces que supe qué podría hacer yo para ayudarla. Yo también iría al centro...pero con una sorpresa especial.

I TOLD MY IDEA to my abuelita and to Miss Lopez. Then I talked to my class and asked all the kids to help. And together, we painted signs for the marchers.

My favorite sign was the one I painted in the brightest colors of all—

I love my Mamá! She is a janitor!

LES CONTÉ MI IDEA a mi abuelita y a la señorita López. Entonces hablé con mi clase y les pedí ayuda a todos los niños. Y juntos, pintamos carteles para los huelguistas.

Mi cartel preferido era el que pinté con los colores más fuertes de todos:

I love my Mamá! She is a janitor!

21

THE NEXT DAY Miss Lopez took some of the kids from my class on the bus to downtown Los Angeles. When Mamá saw us, she was so happy she almost cried. As we marched, I held my sign as high as I could. An old man was playing the accordion. Maria's father took a trash can and played it like a big steel drum. Mamá held soda cans filled with beans and shook them to the beat of the music. On the sidewalk, people rooted for all of us marchers on the street. There were thousands and thousands of people all around me! I held on tight to Miss Lopez' hand.

"Carlos," she said, "this is a celebration of courage."

After three long weeks, the strike was over. My mamá and the janitors finally got the respect and the pay raises they deserved.

"Carlitos," Mamá said, "I couldn't have done it without you." She hung the sign I made on our living room wall. "It's the most beautiful sign in the world," she said.

AL DÍA SIGUIENTE la señorita López llevó a algunos de los chicos de mi clase por autobús al centro de Los Ángeles. Cuando mamá nos vio, se puso tan contenta que casi lloraba. Mientras marchábamos, alcé mi letrero tan alto como pude. Un viejo tocaba el acordeón. El papá de María agarró un basurero y lo tocaba como si fuera un tambor enorme de acero. Mamá llevaba latas para refrescos llenas de frijoles duros y las sonaba al compás de la música. En la acera, la gente nos animaba a todos los manifestantes en la calle. Había miles y miles de gente a mi alrededor. Apreté fuerte la mano de la señorita López.

—Carlos —dijo—, esto es una celebración al valor.

Después de tres largas semanas, se terminó la huelga. Mi mamá y los trabajadores de limpieza por fin recibieron el respeto y los aumentos que merecían.

—Carlitos—dijo mamá—, no pude haberlo hecho sin ti.—Colocó el cartel que hice en la pared de la sala. —Es el cartel más bonito del mundo—dijo.

THAT NIGHT, as always, my mamá tucked me into bed. "Sleep with the angels, Carlitos."

"See you in the morning," I said and closed my eyes.

And that night I had a dream....

When my mamá took the bus to scrub, mop and polish in the tall glass office buildings that shoot up from the streets, I dreamt that angels came down to Los Angeles and sang songs to her while she worked.

ESA NOCHE, como siempre, mi mamá me tapó con las cobijas.

—Que sueñes con los angelitos, Carlitos.

—Hasta mañana—dije y cerré los ojos.

Y esa noche tuve un sueño…

Cuando mi mamá tomó el camión para fregar, limpiar y pulir en los altos edificios de oficinas de vidrio que se alzan de las calles, soñé que unos ángeles bajaron a Los Ángeles y le cantaban canciones mientras trabajaba.

NOW MY MAMÁ SMILES a whole lot more. Abuelita's sore bones feel so much better. She walks with Mamá and me to the school bus in the morning. Mamá no longer has to clean houses and wash clothes on the weekends. Instead, we go to the park and on our way home, she lets me buy a paleta or a churro from the man who sells sweets on the corner.

AHORA MI MAMÁ SE SONRÍE mucho más. Los huesos de mi abuelita ya no le duelen tanto. Nos acompaña a mí y a mamá a la parada del autobus escolar por la mañana. Mamá ya no tiene que limpiar casas y lavar ropa los fines de semana. En vez de eso, vamos al parque y de regreso me deja comprar una paleta o un churro del vendedor de dulces en la esquina.

ONE SATURDAY MORNING the phone rang right after we got home from the park.

"I'll be there," Mamá said before she hung up.

"Carlitos," she said, "I have a promise I must keep: to be there when other workers need my help."

"Who needs your help, Mamá?" I asked.

"People who clean hotel rooms. So this afternoon I am going to meet them."

But just as she was about to leave, I said, "Mamá, wait."

I took down my sign from the living room wall and walked out with her. That afternoon, we joined the workers and marched up and down in front of the hotel. Mamá and I met lots of new friends. And together we shouted, "SÍ, SE PUEDE!"

UN SÁBADO POR LA MAÑANA sonó el teléfono justo al volver del parque.

—Ya voy—dijo mamá antes de cortar la comunicación.

—Carlitos—dijo—, hice una promesa que debo cumplir: apoyar a los otros trabajadores que necesiten de mi ayuda.

—¿Quién necesita de tu ayuda, mamá?—le pregunté.

—Los trabajadores que limpian las habitaciones de hoteles. Pues esta tarde voy para estar con ellos.

Pero justo cuando ella estaba por salir, le dije:—Mamá, espera.

Bajé mi cartel de la pared de la sala y salí con ella. Esa tarde nos juntamos con los trabajadores y marchamos de un lado para otro delante del hotel. Mamá y yo conocimos a muchos amigos nuevos. Y todos juntos gritamos:—¡SÍ, SE PUEDE!

29

A Woman of Struggle, A Woman of Hope

DOLORES SÁNCHEZ is a small woman with a big heart. Gracious and polite, she is a strong woman who knows what she wants. While others go about their business, and perhaps find time to relax, Dolores rushes from home to union hall, from babies to angry union members, to make her day valued—she is a union organizer and mother during the day, and a janitor of office buildings at night. And, like the mother of Carlitos in *¡Sí, Se Puede! / Yes We Can!*, she was a leader in the victorious Los Angeles Justice for Janitors Campaign in April 2000. At 37, Dolores has lived a full life—growing up in the tough streets of Mexico City, risking danger and persecution as a migrant, and now as a working mother and an organizer for the Service Employees International Union, AFL-CIO.

I met Dolores in her well-kept but sparse apartment in the poor immigrant community of Westlake in Los Angeles. While raising three children, one of them an infant, she devotes hours to the union's fight for decent pay and respect for janitors. She reminded me of my own mother, Maria Estela, who worked years in the garment industry or cleaning homes while trying to raise her four children. My father—despite being a principal in Mexico—retired in the U.S. as a laboratory custodian. They came here more than 45 years ago. Millions of their compatriots have come since then. One of those millions is Dolores.

Dolores first arrived in the United States ten years ago. Her first jobs were cleaning offices. It was also around this time that she joined the union. "There are many laws that protect the rich in this country," she says. "We need laws to protect the poor, the working people. The bosses here have all the rights. But workers have nothing to protect them. That's why I joined the union." And that's why she also became active in political campaigns, working toward the election of decent representation for workers and immigrants. "Even if some of us can't vote, we walk the streets to help elect representatives who can pass laws beneficial to workers," she explains.

While being a union activist has taken her away from her home and children, Dolores makes sure they understand why she's

by LUIS J. RODRÍGUEZ

A son of Mexican immigrants, LUIS J. RODRÍGUEZ is an acclaimed author of books of poetry, children's literature, memoir, nonfiction, and short stories. He is also a former steelworker, carpenter, truckdriver, foundry worker and union organizer.

in the union. "I want to show my children that their mother can fight for something better for them," she emphasizes. "But it takes a lot of time. I get home around 3 in the morning, and then I have to get up at 8 to do a few errands. Around noon, I'm at the union hall helping in whatever way I can. After that I return to make dinner just before I go to work. My life is the union, my job, and my home. It's difficult, but any good thing has to be obtained through struggle. There are times I get tired, demoralized, but then I think about what we've achieved. I've learned many things. As a woman, I've gained a lot. For example, I feel more independent. So despite the struggles, it's worth it."

Dolores is married to a man who she says is supportive. And her children also support her. "They know how much the union means to me," Dolores says while going to the kitchen to stir food cooking on the stove. "When I'm in a bad mood, they even tell me, 'Mami, go to the union hall.' They know I need this to have purpose and meaning in my life. And they know how it has made a better life for them."

"And what are the benefits?" I ask.

It doesn't take her long to answer. She says her pay is better than that of the people who toil in industries without unions. They also get good political representation, which she believes is important to impact what happens in this country. "We've been able to obtain a measure of respect from office holders, the owners of the businesses we work for, and the community," she explains. "They see us as an example of how workers should unite, and how by being united we can be strong—every person going their own way just doesn't work."

Most importantly, the union has helped janitors win health insurance—including dental care, eye care, and regular checkups. "This is the most important benefit," she says. "Except for the baby, my children couldn't get Medicare since they weren't born here. We needed health insurance more than anything else."

No wonder Dolores envisions a future when all companies, all businesses become unionized—one hundred percent union labor. Despite claims by many owners that they don't have money, she knows they do. "In the offices, they raise their rents," she explains. "Many of these offices are full. They get big money for being owners of those buildings. This is what I see. So we're prepared to organize so that in the future, we can give our children more security, more opportunity. It's important that the young learn not to let anyone trample over them, not to let anyone humiliate them. I want my children to know how to be strong in a union."

And, from what I can see, their best example is their mother—a strong union woman.

FOR ANN—D.C.

TO MY MOTHER MARIA, MY WIFE BARBARA AND MY SON PEDRO.—F.D.

Cinco Puntos Press

Visit us at
www.cincopuntos.com

Translated by Sharon Franco

Book and jacket design by
Vicki Trego Hill
of El Paso, Texas.

CINCO PUNTOS thanks
David Romo and Ana Lisa Portillo
for their fronterizo read.
Thanks to María Cristina López
for her edit of the Spanish
& thanks to Juan Hernandez
for keeping CPP clean!

ACKNOWLEDGMENTS

A VERY SPECIAL THANKS TO: the janitors of Service Employees International Union (SEIU) 1877 in Los Angeles, especially Dolores Sánchez, Angela Cardona, Natalia Rodríguez and her grandson Chris Rodríguez, Edith Portillo and her son Jesse Portillo, Blanca Perez, Julio Morales and his daughters Sylvia Natalie Morales and Ivonne Natalie Morales, who shared their stories with us and reviewed this manuscript.

JARS OF HONEY FOR: Ann Bastian, Madeline Janis-Aparicio, Peter Cervantes-Gautschi, Janet Shenk, Susan Sully, Colin Greer, Jono Shaffer, Triana Silton, Blanca Galleagos, Christina Roessler, Alison Barlow, Diego Iriarte, Mary Grillo, Donald Cohen, Amy Dean, Karen Byrne, Cora Weiss, Jennifer Beckman, Harriet Barlow, Sara Wendt, Ada Sanchez, Juana Ponce de Leon, Craig Merrilees, Luis Rodriguez, Carolyn Cohen, Paul Hawken, Greg Ruggerio, Scott Tremiel, and Bobby and Lee Byrd for their generosity in cross pollinating ideas and support.

LOAVES OF FRESH BREAD FOR: Lance Lindblom, Anannya Bhattacharjee, Victor Quintana, Margy Fine, Harold Meyerson, Beata Pudelko, Karla Zombro, Chuck Shufford, Janet Lansberry, Amy Martyn, Kerrie LePlante, Martha Eddy, Marianne Monoc, Anita Nager. Rosa Paredes, Jody Quirk, Richard Healey, Lucy Greer, Susan Cohn-Schulz, Angela Thompson, John Cavanagh, Marion and Alan Hunt-Badiner, David Rosenmiller, Chelo Alvarez, Anjana Shakya, Deko Menishian, Mary Woltz, and Andrew Bachmann for helping this project rise and take form.

BOUQUETS OF ROSES FOR: The New World Foundation, Unitarian Universalist Veatch Program at Shelter Rock, Solidago Foundation, Samuel Rubin Foundation, Needmor Fund, French American Charitable Trust, Nathan Cummings Foundation, Lawson Valentine Foundation, McKay Foundation, Blue Mountain Center, Threshold Foundation, Lowwood Foundation, New Visions Foundation, Alan and Andrea Rabinowitz, National Interfaith Committee for Worker Justice, Jobs With Justice, Service Employees International Union and Cinco Puntos Press for their support which made this project blossom and made complimentary copies available for workers and their families.

Printed in Hong Kong by Morris Printing. FIRST EDITION 10 9 8 7 6 5 4 3 2 1
Library of Congress Cataloging-in-Publication Data. Cohn, Diana. ¡Sí, se puede! Yes, we can! by Diana Cohn ; illustrated by Francisco Delgado. p. cm.   ISBN 0-938317-66-0   I. Title: Yes, we can!. II. Delgado, Francisco, 1974- ill. III. Title.   PZ73 .C583 2002   [E]—dc21   2002002326